The Adventures
of
Mantee
the Praying Mantis

ISBN 979-8-88832-694-7 (paperback)
ISBN 979-8-88751-101-6 (hardcover)
ISBN 979-8-88751-100-9 (digital)

Christian Faith Publishing
832 Park Avenue
Meadville, PA 16335
www.christianfaithpublishing.com

Bible excerpts are from the public domain King James Version from biblegateway.com.

Printed in the United States of America

The Adventures
of
Mantee
the Praying Mantis

Candy Walcott

Illustrated by Deborah DeHart

Heartfelt thanks to Mrs. Gloria Burleson; Linda Gilman; my husband, Vinod; and the Holy Spirit for the inspiration.

Mantee was born in a beautiful garden, and he lived
with all his brothers and sisters in a bright flowerpot.
This was located on the family garden patio.

One bright spring day, Mantee and his brothers and sisters
were old enough to come out of their flowerpot and climb
onto the table and get a really good view of the garden.

3

All of a sudden, they saw another creature towering above them, sitting at the patio table. It was a real, live human being.

It was a lady named Mrs. Holly. She was reading her Bible and praying,

They were very still as they heard a peaceful prayer coming from Mrs. Holly. Mantee drew closer and thought, *What is this? How do you pray?*

As he sat on the back of the chair, he heard her softly say,

"Our Father which art in heaven, Hallowed be thy name. Thy kingdom come, Thy will be done in earth, as it is in heaven. Give us this day our daily bread. And forgive us our debts, as we forgive our debtors. And lead us not into temptation, but deliver us from evil: For thine is the kingdom, and the power, and the glory, for ever. Amen" (Matthew 6:9–13).

Mantee thought, *Wow! What a cool idea.*

As he sat listening to the lady, he didn't notice that his brothers and sisters sounded farther and farther away. You see, that day was very special to the praying mantis family. The time had come for them to explore the world on their own.

Mantee was different. He was
so happy in the garden. He thought,
No way! I am not leaving!

Mrs. Holly closed her Bible, and Mantee decided to return to his
home in the flowerpot. His mother was really surprised to see him.
She said, "Mantee, it is time for you to go and see the world."
He replied, "Mom, no. I can learn so much right here. Guess
what I learned today? I learned how to pray, and when I saw the
lady outside the flowerpot, she folded her hands to pray."
Mantee's mom said, "That is very exciting, but you have not
started your journey and all your brothers and sisters left
the flowerpot today. You have to start your journey."
Mantee replied, "Yes, Mom. I will start tomorrow, but I really love it here."

Mantee was so sad that night. As he was lying in bed, he thought, *I do not want to leave. Maybe if I pray like Mrs. Holly, I might get to stay here.*

13

Mantee started the Lord's Prayer,

"Our Father which art in heaven, Hallowed be thy name. Thy kingdom come, Thy will be done in earth, as it is in heaven. Give us this day our daily bread. And forgive us our debts, as we forgive our debtors. And lead us not into temptation, but deliver us from evil: For thine is the kingdom, and the power, and the glory, for ever. Amen" (Matthew 6:9–13).

Mantee slept that night with his little arms folded across his
chest. Early the next morning, Mantee hurried out of the flowerpot,
hoping to hear the lady again. Sure enough, Mrs. Holly was in
her usual chair, and Mantee listened as she started praying.

"Our Father which art in heaven, Hallowed be thy name. Thy kingdom
come, Thy will be done in earth, as it is in heaven. Give us this day our
daily bread. And forgive us our debts, as we forgive our debtors. And lead
us not into temptation, but deliver us from evil: For thine is the kingdom,
and the power, and the glory, for ever. Amen" (Matthew 6:9–13).

That morning, Mantee caught more food than anybody else in the garden. As he went back to the flowerpot that afternoon, he saw his mother and knew she would be upset with him for not finding his own flowerpot that day.

To Mantee's surprise, his mom had heard how much food he got that
day. She asked, "Mantee, how in the world did you catch all that food?"
Mantee said, "Mom, I know it is the prayer I learned
from the lady. It was so easy to catch food."

18

Mantee's mother and father were so proud of their son, yet his mom and dad knew it was time for Mantee to venture out on his own. His mother said, "Mantee, would you please teach us how to pray?"

Mantee replied, "Oh yes, Mom. I would love to",
Mantee began to recite the Lord's Prayer.

"Our Father which art in heaven, Hallowed be thy name. Thy kingdom come, Thy will be done in earth, as it is in heaven. Give us this day our daily bread. And forgive us our debts, as we forgive our debtors. And lead us not into temptation, but deliver us from evil: For thine is the kingdom, and the power, and the glory, for ever. Amen" (Matthew 6:9–13).

Mantee prayed again that night for his very own flowerpot.
The next morning, Mantee got up early to start his journey.
Something caught his eye in the far corner of the patio. It was
a bright blue flowerpot. Mantee's prayers were answered!

Mantee smiled a huge smile as he stared
across the patio at the new blue pot the
lady had just put out the night before.

Mantee was on his way to his very own

adventures in his own backyard.

The End

About the Author

Candy Walcott is a Desert Storm veteran and a native Texan. She was inspired by her pet-sitting business to write the column Pet Nanny for the *Loop* newspaper in Tehachapi, California. The column focused on heartwarming and funny stories about her adventures as a pet sitter.

Candy has a passion for nature and animals and loves to create stories teaching children scriptures and life lessons. Currently, she resides in Fort Worth, Texas, with her husband and cats. She also enjoys fostering cats with Saving Hope Rescue.